# How

MW01005181

# youth retreat

Stephen & Shae Pepper

Youth Workin' It

# CONTENTS

# INTRODUCTION

Thank you for buying 'How to plan a youth retreat' – we hope you'll find it as useful as we think it will be.

We know that planning a youth retreat takes a lot of organization and preparation, so this book takes you through the different stages step-by-step. It breaks down areas like the youth retreat budget, helping you to create an affordable – and accurate – budget.

Many youth retreats are run by churches, but we know other organizations and charities also run retreats. We've therefore tried to make this book applicable to all types of youth retreats as much as possible, whether they're faith-based or not. You'll notice some small sections titled "Cross Culture" though – these are extra thoughts more relevant to churches that are running a youth retreat.

This book isn't all you get though. Throughout "How to Plan a Youth Retreat", we mention various different documents – Budget Tables, Parent Cost Feedback forms, Parental Consent forms, Risk Assessments, etc. These are all important and useful resources when planning a youth retreat, so we wanted to make them available to you as an added bonus for buying this book.

We've therefore produced these as Word and Excel documents for you to be able to download and print off yourself. This means you can amend these documents so that they're individually tailored for your youth retreat.

When these free forms and templates are mentioned in the book, they are shown in bold, italicized and underlined, e.g. ***Budget Table***

How do you get these free sample templates? Easy – just send an email to retreat@youthworkinit.com. You'll receive an automated reply providing a link to download all of these documents.

# 1

# WHY RUN A YOUTH RETREAT?

Before you start planning the youth retreat, ask yourself, **"What do we want to achieve with this retreat?"**

Some find it helpful to work in a group setting so they can bounce ideas off each other. If this is you, sit down with 1-2 key volunteers or trusted youth worker friends and/or colleagues.

You may find that you only have one objective, or it might be that you have several. Either way, here is a list of some reasons to run a youth retreat:

### 1) There's a theme you want to cover over a weekend

Sometimes in your youth work, you'll want to be able to go much deeper on a subject that's just not possible in a one hour session. A youth retreat gives you the chance to focus on this subject over an entire weekend.

## 2) Youth get a stronger faith while on a retreat

If your retreat is faith-based, you might have found that away from the hustle and bustle of their normal lives, your youth develop a deeper relationship with God.

## 3) You have a number of new youth in your group

A youth retreat gives a fantastic opportunity for the new young people to be integrated with the existing group, with relationships being built much more quickly than would happen normally.

## 4) You have a new youth pastor, youth workers or volunteers

Similar to point 3, a retreat is also a great chance for new staff or volunteers to get to know the youth.

## 5) You want to get to know the youth more

Even if you've led the youth group for a long time, you'll get to know the young people in a completely different way over the course of a weekend (or however long your retreat is), than you do seeing them for just a couple of hours each week.

## 6) You run a retreat every year

If your church or organization runs a youth retreat every year, the students would be disappointed if there wasn't one.

## 7) You want to organize something fun the youth can invite their friends to

Your young people might be more willing to invite their friends to a youth retreat than to other events. This will help integrate their friends in the group and make them more likely to remain involved after the retreat.

## 8) You want to celebrate something

Maybe your young people are graduating high school or have run a successful event. Either way, a youth retreat could be a chance to celebrate their achievements.

## 9) Your youth are from low-income families

If you work with young people from low-income families, they may never be given an opportunity to get away. A youth retreat therefore gives them a chance to experience something new.

## 10) You want to book a guest speaker

There might be a person you'd like to come to speak to your youth group, but an hour isn't long enough. A youth retreat gives the guest speaker a much longer opportunity to feed into the lives of your youth.

~

If you and your volunteers have a clear aim of what you want to achieve, you'll be a lot more focused on what's needed to make the youth retreat a success.

It'll give you a clearer idea of what kind of retreat center to book, how much it'll cost, what activities you can do and how you should promote it.

Having a vision of what you want to achieve means parents will be more supportive, as you'll be able to tell them how their children will benefit from the time away (and who doesn't need more supportive parents!)

Knowing what you want to achieve will also help you when recruiting volunteers, as you'll have a vision you can inspire them with.

**_Action Point:_**

- _Identify why you want to run a youth retreat_

# 2

# RECRUITING AND MANAGING VOLUNTEERS

This may seem like a strange chapter to have so early in the book, but there are good reasons for this:

*When you consider volunteer recruitment and management at an early stage in the planning process, the preparation will become infinitely easier, the retreat will be better and your volunteers will be more committed.*

## VOLUNTEER RECRUITMENT

Maybe you're an independent person and find it hard to include others when planning or delegating tasks to others. Planning the youth retreat by yourself means that everything is done exactly how you want it.

Resist this approach!

Being the sole person in charge of planning a youth retreat may seem like a good idea, but there are good reasons to involve your volunteers in the planning from the outset.

### 1) Extra ideas

The more people there are involved in the planning of the youth retreat, the more ideas there are that can get suggested. This will give you a much better selection of ideas to choose from, hopefully resulting in a more fun and better organized retreat.

This doesn't mean you have to accept everyone's idea or have majority voting on all the planning areas – you can still be the person in charge of making final decisions. However, get as much input as possible.

### 2) Gets people committed at an early stage

If you involve volunteers in the decision-making process at an early stage, this will give them buy-in and result in volunteers who are more committed. They'll also be far more likely to turn up to youth retreat planning meetings if they know they'll have a say in what will happen at the retreat.

### 3) Shows what they're passionate about

The youth retreat ideas that your volunteers come up with will most likely relate to the areas that they're passionate about. This not only helps you to get to know your volunteers better, but it also......

## 4) Helps with delegating

The areas that your volunteers are passionate about are also likely to be the areas that they are most keen to help with leading up to (and at) the youth retreat. This makes it easier to delegate tasks, which in turn......

## 5) Lightens your workload

Organizing a youth retreat means that you'll have a much higher workload on top of whatever your normal job is – whether you're a full-time youth pastor/youth worker or someone who does youth work in their free time. Getting your volunteers involved in coming up with youth retreat ideas and planning for it will lighten your workload, making your life easier and stress-free.

~

Most of the time, the people who help at a youth retreat are the same people who volunteer to work with the youth normally. However, there are many other people who may have something they can contribute to the youth retreat (this can include youth – for more information see Chapter 8) – even those who don't want to do any youth work.

Youth retreat volunteers that don't want to work with youth. Sounds strange? It doesn't have to be. At one camp I ran, a lady from my church wanted to support the work we were doing with disadvantaged youth from inner-city London. She sponsored a place for a young person on the camp, plus offered her services as a cook for the whole week.

There are actually many areas where people with certain skills and/or resources can help, without requiring them to work with youth – here are some to get you started:

## 1) Cooks

Depending on the retreat center that you book, meals might not be included. Although this may save money, it does mean that you need people who can prepare meals for everybody at the youth retreat.

Instead of having your volunteers double up as chefs, are there people you could ask who would be willing to be a cook? They wouldn't have to be involved with the youth work (unless they wanted to be), so they might enjoy still being able to contribute to the running of the youth retreat.

## 2) Website designer

A website can be a great way to provide information to youth and their parents about the youth retreat. If you're not skilled in creating websites, chances are that there's somebody you know who can set one up for you. Websites can even be created for free – it's simple and easy to do, even if you don't have any experience designing websites.

One of our next books is going to detail how to create a youth group website. The guide in that book can therefore easily be used to learn how to create a youth retreat website.

### 3) Video maker/editor
Videos are another great way of generating interest in the youth retreat. If you've got video footage from past youth retreats, find someone who can edit videos so that you can make a montage showing how much fun the retreats are. The videos can then be shown in your church, youth club, community center, etc, as well as being uploaded to Youtube and directing people there. Most website templates enable you to embed Youtube videos easily, so the videos could also be added to the youth retreat website (see point 2).

### 4) Graphic designer
If you're not creative and artsy, there's a good chance that the flyers and/or leaflets you produce to promote the youth retreat aren't going to be particularly exciting. Graphic designers can help you create a vibrant youth retreat flyer that doesn't have to be expensive.

### 5) Accountant
Budgets aren't for everyone, but they're one of the main things that you'll have to deal with if you're organizing a youth retreat. If numbers aren't your

thing, is there an accountant or treasurer who can help you with the youth retreat budget?

If budgets are your Kryptonite though, chapter 4 is for you.

### 6) First aider

Safety is an important area of the youth retreat to give serious consideration. If you're the main person in charge, we'd highly recommend becoming first aid trained yourself. The Red Cross provides first aid courses all over the country – their website will help you to find one close to you.

However, if neither you nor any of your volunteers are first aid trained and there isn't time to organize this, is there anybody else you know who has this training? They wouldn't necessarily need to be involved with any youth work – you could just ask them if they'd be willing to be on site in case there are any medical issues.

If the retreat center you book is actually more of an activity center, there's a good chance that their staff will be first aid trained, so you may not need to bring along a dedicated first aider.

Don't leave this to chance though – check with the retreat center if their staff are first aid trained and if they'd always be available in an emergency. When checking in at the start of the retreat, get the name and contact details of the relevant person. Also consider providing contact badges for your volunteers, so that they know who to contact if first aid is required.

## 7) Administrator for registration and feedback

Administration isn't everybody's gifting. If paperwork isn't your strong suit, try to identify someone who would be willing to take care of the registration for the youth retreat. They could deal with the registration forms, taking money, providing receipts, etc, freeing you up to focus on other areas.

This person could also be in charge of getting feedback after the youth retreat. Feedback is covered in chapter 11, as it's important to find out what youth, parents and your volunteers thought of the youth retreat and ways in which it could be improved next time.

## 8) Photographer

Having a photographer with a good quality camera at the youth retreat is very beneficial. They can take photos and video footage which can be used for a photo/video montage at the end of the retreat. The photos can also be uploaded to the youth retreat website afterwards, shown to parents to give them an idea of what happened and used to promote the next youth retreat you plan.

In order for you to be able to use the photos for publicity, uploading to websites, etc, you'll need to have the parents sign a ***Photo Release form***. This is one of the free documents you get having bought this book – see the introduction for details on how to get these useful resources.

## 9) Donors or sponsors

If some (or all) of the young people you work with are from low-income families, they might not be able to afford to attend the youth retreat without financial help. Are there any people in your community, church, workplace, etc, who would be willing to sponsor a place on the youth retreat to enable a young person to go?

## 10) Drivers

Youth retreats will often be some distance from your local community. Rather than having parents drop off their children at the retreat center, you may instead wish to have the youth meet at one location in your local area, then transport them all by minibus, minivan, carpool, etc.

If you do things this way, you may need one or more people who are willing to drive a minibus to the retreat center and back again at the end of the youth retreat.

*"This is all well and good, but what happens if I don't have any volunteers to help with the youth work at the youth retreat?"*

This is a good question. If you already have a large team of volunteers, there's a good chance you'll be able to recruit some or all of them to help at the retreat.

If you don't have many volunteers in your youth ministry/youth work organization (or few that are willing to help you run a retreat), one of the best ways to recruit more volunteers is to <u>ask people directly.</u> Some members of your church (or other people you know) may not think that they're equipped to help. Having you ask them personally because you think they have the qualities you need will be more likely to encourage them to volunteer.

When doing this: be **specific**, be **complimentary**, but be **genuine**. The approach could look something like this:

*"Hey Andy. I was chatting to Johnny the other day and he was telling me that you're a great baseball coach. We're planning a youth retreat for the fall where we'll be doing loads of sports and I thought you'd be a great addition to the team. It sounds like the young people you coach really respect you and appreciate how much you care about them, which are exactly the kind of characteristics I'm looking for.*

*Would you therefore be willing to volunteer to help at the retreat by organizing some sports that weekend"*

> *Cross Culture*
> *Another option is to make an announcement in a church service, as this will reach a larger number of potential volunteers.*

Before trying to recruit additional volunteers, take some time to list the activities that you would need them to do; people will be more willing to sign up to help if they have a better idea of what would be expected of them at the youth retreat. If your theme is going to be about poverty, people that work for non-profit organizations might be more likely to get involved. If your theme is about nature, people who work with animals or plants may be keen on sharing their knowledge.

When recruiting additional volunteers for the youth retreat, ask them in a way that casts a vision for what you want to achieve at the retreat, instead of phrasing it negatively. Compare the following:

*1) "Look, we're running a youth retreat in September and I really need some extra volunteers. If no adults offer to help, we're not going to be able to run it and we'll lose our deposit at the retreat center."*

2) *"I'm really excited as we're taking the youth to a retreat center in September for an awesome time of team-building and discovery. The theme's going to be 'Building Healthy Relationships' and I need a few people to help me lead that weekend, as we help the youth learn about something that's so important in their daily lives. I know this sounds exciting to some of you but you might not be sure how you'd be able to help – please come and speak to me after the service. I've got a list of areas we need help with – I'm sure there's something you can offer that would help us speak into the lives of our young people."*

With the first example, you might get a few people offering to help, but they'd probably be doing it out of guilt. If you ask for help in a similar way to the second example though, you're far more likely to get people offering to help who really want to be there at the retreat. The difference in attitude at the retreat will be noticeable as well – youth can tell if adults don't really want to be there.

## VOLUNTEER MANAGEMENT

### Before the retreat

If it's possible to get the volunteers all together at some point, organize a visit to the retreat center once it's been booked so that they can have a look around. This will give them a better idea of what to expect, so if they're organizing any activities or leading any meetings, they'll know the layout of the site, meeting rooms, etc. when they're planning.

*Cross Culture*
*For a church youth retreat, take the opportunity to pray over the site as you walk around.*

This visit can also double as a team bonding day, so even though it may only take an hour to look around the site, try to spend as much time together as possible, even if that just means going for a meal together afterwards.

This visit is also an ideal opportunity to obtain a copy of the retreat center's risk assessment and create your own for any activities that your team will be responsible for. See chapter 9 to learn more about how to perform a risk assessment.

If volunteers will be leading any of the group meetings, let them know at least two months in advance what you'd like them to talk about – this will give them plenty of time to prepare, in case they're too busy in the week or two leading up to the retreat. Keep in touch with the volunteers who will be speaking in the group meetings and ask them for a brief outline of what they'll be talking about – this will ensure that the same subject or Bible story isn't covered by more than one person. Also find out if they'll need anything for what they're planning, such as a DVD player and TV, props for a skit, etc. This can be added to a checklist of things to take to the retreat.

About two or three weeks before the retreat, put together a leadership pack. This will include things like the schedule for the retreat, information about the theme, the duties all the volunteers will have and any preparation that they need to do.

At the retreat, will the youth be breaking off into smaller groups in order to discuss what's been talked about at the group meetings? If so, and if the volunteers will be facilitating those discussions, include some questions in the leadership pack that they can use to get the young people talking.

**During the retreat**

One of the most important things will be to ensure good communication with your leadership team, both before and during the retreat. If you've done most of the planning, you'll have a clear idea of what you want done, but if this isn't communicated to the other leaders then they might end up getting frustrated.

For example, don't assume that they'll all know what to do to set up for the group meetings – give volunteers a list of duties so that they know what's expected of them. It might be a good idea to include diagrams for room set up (e.g. where the stage is, how many small group chair clusters are needed, etc), so that volunteers are able to work independently without your direct supervision.

If any of your volunteers at the retreat aren't normally involved in your youth work, make sure that they often have things to do, even if that's simply playing basketball with the youth. Things that come naturally to more experienced youth workers don't always come naturally to those who are new to it. Giving them some suggestions or guidance on what to do will help them to not feel out of place at the retreat and will mean they feel useful.

If parents will be bringing their children to the retreat, try to have your leadership team arrive at the retreat center some time before the youth are due to arrive. This will give you all enough time to set everything up and have the registration area prepared.

However, if the youth are all meeting somewhere (e.g. your church) beforehand and you've arranged to transport them to the site, this may mean some of the leadership team will be involved in the transportation. If that's the case, still try to have as many of the other leaders on site in time to give the youth a warm welcome when they arrive.

Each night at the retreat, meet together as a leadership team to discuss what went well and what didn't during the day. For things that went well, identify why they went well – was it due to good preparation, good communication, fun activities, etc? Draw on these positives and try to find ways these lessons can be recreated for the remainder of the retreat.

For things that didn't go so well, identify why that was the case – was it poor preparation, poor communication, activities the youth didn't find interesting, etc? Don't have this be a time where people are blamed for things going wrong – these meetings will be late at night and so leaders will be tired and emotions may run high. Instead, resolve to put the negatives behind you and to learn from the experience over the remainder of the retreat.

In the mornings, meet together as a leadership team before the youth get up. Briefly go over the plans for the day and what everyone's duties will be.

> *Cross Culture*
> *After the morning and evening leadership meetings, spend some time in prayer together.*

Throughout the youth retreat, check in with all the different leaders to make sure that they're all doing OK and whether they have anything they need to talk about – they may be more willing to discuss concerns in private rather than in front of all of the other leaders.

Take this opportunity to encourage and praise them as well. Make the praise specific – instead of saying something vague like, "You've been really helpful", say "I really appreciate how you set up the group meeting room, even though that wasn't something that was expected of you". Instead of, "You're doing a great job with the youth", say "I noticed you spent some time talking with Jack when he was feeling homesick. Thanks for taking time out to comfort him rather than ignoring how he was feeling and just hoping he would feel better."

Not only will this greatly encourage your leaders on a personal level, but it will also encourage them to continue doing these great things that you've identified. Make it a point to praise each leader personally at some point during the retreat.

**After the retreat**

Arrange to have a meeting with all of the other leaders to discuss how the retreat went overall – what went well and what could be improved next time. An ideal time to do this would be straight after the youth have gone home, as the retreat will be fresh in everybody's minds and everybody will still be together. This may not work for some of the leaders though, as they may have other commitments to attend to. If that's the case, try to arrange a meeting for some time within the next week. A meeting a few days after the retreat can be a good time, as the leaders will have had time to rest and reflect on the youth retreat, perhaps bringing some extra clarity of thought and insight into how the retreat went.

If any of the leaders on the retreat aren't part of your regular youth work team and you think they would be a good addition to your team, discuss with them whether they would like to start getting more involved. They may have really enjoyed their experience on the retreat and so could be interested in continuing to build relationships with the youth they met there.

Once you have a better idea of why you want to run a youth retreat and who your volunteers will be, you'll be able to start working on a youth retreat theme and aim.

### *Action Points:*

- *Identify and recruit volunteers for the retreat as soon as possible*
- *Involve people who have anything to offer*
- *Include volunteers in planning process*
- *Communicate well before, during and after the retreat*

# 3

# THEMES, AIMS AND OBJECTIVES

You've sat down and worked out the reason(s) you want to run a youth retreat. You've started recruiting volunteers for the retreat. It's now time to put these together by choosing a theme and setting aims and objectives for the retreat.

What's the difference between a theme, an aim and an objective? A theme is *the subject you'll be covering during the youth retreat*. An aim is *what you want to achieve (like the goal, and is often broad)* and an objective is *how you plan to achieve the aim (this is very specific and measureable)*.

Choosing your youth retreat theme early in the planning process and creating clear aims and objectives will actually help with the rest of the planning. How so? Consider the following things you'll organize and how knowing your youth retreat theme, aims and objectives will assist in these areas:

## 1) Retreat center location
If you choose a theme about nature, creation, etc, for your youth retreat, booking a retreat center in

the mountains or a forest will help tie in with that theme, rather than booking a center not surrounded by nature. If your aim relates to team-building, a retreat center that offers a lot of group activities will facilitate that.

> *Cross Culture*
> *If your youth retreat is run by a church, you may choose to use your own building to reduce the cost of the retreat. Also consider partnering with another church (perhaps within your denomination or movement) where you can use their venue, as you would your own, but with the benefit of being in a different location.*

## 2) Helpers

Knowing your youth retreat theme, aims and objectives upfront means potential helpers can see that you're well organized and will have more confidence in your leadership. As mentioned in the second chapter, it can also be a good idea to include your helpers when choosing an aim and theme for the youth retreat in the first place. That gives them an opportunity to give their own suggestions, which in turn helps them to feel more included in the planning and provides a sense of ownership.

## 3) Parents

If you haven't chosen a theme, or any clear goals or reasons for running the retreat, and parents ask what the youth retreat is about, you might struggle for an answer. Therefore, having an aim and theme nailed down before speaking to parents about the youth retreat will give them greater confidence in your abilities – something youth workers and youth pastors always welcome!

## 4) Budget

The largest part of a youth retreat budget tends to be allocated to paying for the retreat center. As your theme, aims and objectives can affect which retreat center you use (see point 1), it can in turn affect your budget. Depending on your youth retreat theme and aims, you may also need to purchase additional resources which further affect your budget. It's therefore best to know this upfront, rather than having several unplanned expenses further down the line.

## 5) Activities

Once you've chosen a theme, created clear aims and laid out how you want to achieve them, you can start planning discussions, small groups, activities and games that relate to them.

~

Choosing aims and defining their objectives may be the first thing you do when planning a retreat. Or you may already know what you want to achieve, even if you haven't mapped it out in great detail. Choosing your aims and a theme are often interchangeable steps in the planning process, depending on your reasons for running the retreat as identified in Chapter 1. First, we're going to discuss how to choose a theme and then explore creating aims and objectives. However you can skip to the section about aims and objectives and then come back to identifying a theme depending on the needs of your planning process.

**CHOOSING A THEME**

As mentioned previously, involving your volunteers in this kind of decision is a good idea, as they may have suggestions you haven't thought of. However, if you want to pick a youth retreat theme that speaks into the lives of your young people, what better way to do this than by asking the youth themselves what issues are important to them?

You may be dubious about involving the young people in this way, but here are some reasons why it's a good idea to get youth involvement with decisions such as these:

**Makes it relevant**
Having your young people pick the youth retreat theme will help ensure that it's about something important to them.

**Provides insight**
By asking the students to help pick a theme, it'll give you an idea as to what things they're interested in or areas that they're struggling with. Either way, it's a good opportunity to get your youth to share their feelings in a non-threatening way.

**Gives ideas for the future**
If you've allowed the young people to pick any theme they want without giving them any suggestions, you'll get a wide range of subjects they want to learn more about. This therefore provides a good list of other topics to cover when you get back from the youth retreat.

**Makes them feel valued**
By asking them what they want the youth retreat theme to be, your young people will feel more empowered and that you care about what they think, helping you build a trusting relationship with them.

This doesn't mean that you have to allow the youth to make all the decisions or even the final decision. This process should be a partnership between youth, with great and valid ideas, and the adults in their lives who have important experiences and a wider understanding of the larger context of the entire retreat and youth program.

## Shortlisting retreat theme ideas

When asking young people to help pick a youth retreat theme, you could give them a list of themes to choose from or leave it completely open to have them give their own ideas.

Giving a list means that you don't spend an entire session getting dozens of completely random suggestions and helps guide their thoughts. However, allowing them to be free to choose anything will give you more ideas for the future and more insight into issues in their lives.

There are a few different methods for getting youth to give ideas, as well as to narrow down the ideas to a final 3 – 5. You can repeat the process until you get down to the final theme. There are different methods for generating and narrowing down the ideas, some are more traditional and some are more 'techie', so use the method that works best based on your group's age, size and access to technology. Here are four ideas:

## 1) Hold a discussion and 'shout out' ideas
If you have a small group (or a large group you've separated into smaller groups) you can have them

discuss possible ideas and make a list of retreat theme topics by shouting out their ideas. You will need to facilitate the group well to make sure that even quiet or shy youth have their ideas and opinions heard.

**2) Show of hands**
Although this can be quick and easy, it has a drawback. Youth can be influenced quite easily by what their friends think, so they might be too embarrassed to put up their hand for an option like sex.

They might also wait to see what the most popular youth pick and choose that as well, rather than going for the option they really want.

**3) Paper**
Instead of asking for a show of hands, give each of them a piece of paper and ask them to offer their suggestions. To ensure you get truly honest answers, make sure the youth are sitting reasonably far apart and give them all the same colored pen.

Sitting them apart will mean they don't have to worry about others reading what they've written. Giving them all the same colored pen will mean they won't be so concerned about you identifying what their choices are based on the color they've written in. Once they've written down their ideas, have them fold their piece of paper and put it in a bowl.

## 4) Online survey

You can set up free surveys online at Survey Monkey and email all the young people the link, as well as putting the link on your website, your youth group's Facebook page and Tweeted out (depending on if you use any or all these forms of media).

If you don't currently use social media in your youth work, check out the "Social Media" tag on http://youthworkinit.com/blog for guides on how to get started.

Online surveys have the benefit of true anonymity, so youth may like picking a youth retreat theme this way. One drawback is that you might get less engagement than you would if you incorporated choosing the youth retreat theme into a youth work session. To ensure maximum engagement, try to have a computer set up for use during the session where they can complete the survey.

~

You might be in a position where your youth retreat is in the next few weeks and you need to decide on a theme as soon as possible. To help you out, there's a list below of 45 youth retreat themes that can be used whether your retreat is faith-based or not. Below that, there's a Cross Culture section with a further 40 themes churches may wish to use.

1. Poverty
2. Self-image
3. Dating
4. Forgiveness
5. Bullying
6. Relationships
7. Love
8. Peer pressure
9. Peace
10. Kindness
11. Persecution
12. Integrity
13. Families
14. Hope
15. Joy
16. Substance abuse
17. Physical health
18. Patience
19. Worry
20. Serving others
21. Christmas
22. Service trips
23. Sex
24. Global issues
25. Internet
26. Accountability
27. Self-control
28. Confidence
29. Money
30. Grace
31. Gossip

32. School
33. Making decisions
34. Justice
35. Temptation
36. Anger management
37. Reconciliation
38. Honesty
39. Team building
40. Making a difference
41. Loyalty
42. Friends
43. Setting up a Youth Council
44. Life skills
45. The environment

*Cross Culture*

*While many of the themes above can also easily be used within the church, here are some specific faith-based programming theme ideas:*

1. Faith
2. Heaven
3. Doubt
4. Holiness
5. Treasures in heaven
6. The Ten Commandments
7. Fruits of the Spirit
8. Prayer

9.  The Trinity
10. Small groups
11. Character from the Bible
12. Your body is a temple
13. Sermon on the Mount
14. Spiritual gifts
15. Sin
16. One body, many parts
17. Evangelism
18. Baptism
19. Resurrection
20. Jesus
21. Salvation
22. Creation
23. Worship
24. A book of the Bible
25. A chapter in the Bible
26. Parables
27. Following God's directions
28. Communion
29. Easter
30. Miracles
31. Reading the Bible
32. Holy Spirit
33. Doing devotions
34. False idols

35. Tithing
36. Mission Trips
37. The Good Samaritan
38. Life and Death of a Disciple
39. Women of the Bible
40. Men of the Bible

As we've already mentioned, choosing a youth retreat theme early on in the planning process is a good idea. So is identifying a goal(s) for the retreat as a whole and creating objectives so you know when and how you've achieved your aims. Remember, aims are the goal, while objectives are how you'll know you've achieved your goal.

However, there's not just one aim and one objective for the entire planning process – they are important throughout. For example, you should have one to three large aims for your retreat and they'll each have one or more objectives. Then you'll have more specific aims relating to each day, session or activity and objectives for them. You will have aims for your volunteers, your youth, yourself and objectives for each of those. You may even have some aims for when the retreat ends (in relation to your ongoing youth programs) and objectives for that. Everything you do should have an aim and an objective.

Often, we don't plan out in great detail; however, taking the time early on to thoroughly plan and identify the aims and their objectives will help you in the long run. You'll know the purpose of all the activities on your retreat and you'll be able to give an account of how the money has been spent to parents, donors and other stakeholders. It will help provide evidence for your methods, not only making you a better practitioner but by also providing important statistical information to possible future donors. This will make your program more fundable, sustainable and replicable if that is a long term goal of your program or organization.

## AIMS

Aims are just goals. They're what you want to get out of the retreat. You may have many different goals. You may have one related to youth growth, one for volunteer development, one for attendance, etc.

For example, you may want your youth to have a better understanding of global issues by the end of the retreat. Or you may want to recruit new volunteers for your weekly programming after they helped on the retreat. Or you want more youth at this year's retreat than last year's.

All you do at this stage is make a list of all the things you want to accomplish as a result of this retreat. You may want to choose three as your primary aims for the retreat so that when people ask, you don't give them a list of fifteen things.

See if your volunteers – and possibly your youth as well – have any goals they would like to achieve by the end of the retreat. Perhaps your volunteers want to get more confident when talking to young people. Or your youth want to learn how to canoe. Whatever it is, have them list the goals they have for the retreat too.

## OBJECTIVES

Objectives are more specific than aims. They take the idea you have in your goal and make it something you can measure. They make it **SMART**.

This might be a term you've come across before, but if not, the acronym stands for:

**S**pecific
**M**easurable
**A**chievable
**R**elevant
**T**ime-based

We'll go through each of these stages to help you create a SMART youth retreat aim.

### Specific

Why does your objective need to be specific? Because how else will you know if you've achieved it by the end of the youth retreat?

If your aim is "We want the young people to have a good time on the youth retreat", you're not being particularly specific and different people could interpret it in different ways. Would it mean they enjoy just one activity, or every single activity? Does it mean every young person has to enjoy the retreat?

A good way of making sure your youth retreat objective is specific is by asking yourself about the Ws:

- **WHAT** are you wanting to achieve? This ties in with the first chapter.
- **WHO** is the aim impacting? This would generally be the young people, but you may have an aim for your volunteers too.
- **WHEN** is the aim related to? Usually it would be at the youth retreat, but perhaps your aim is actually related to what happens *after* the retreat.
- **WHERE** are you wanting to achieve the aim? Again, most of the time it would be at the youth retreat, but maybe it'll be related to when the youth are back home.
- **WHY** are you wanting to achieve the aim?

**Measurable**

When you're making an objective, you need to ensure that there's a way of measuring whether or not you've achieved it. This will oftentimes relate to the number of youth – perhaps you want at least 10 students to agree to join a small group after the youth retreat.

The measurement might instead be a percentage – that you want 95% of the young people to complete a certain activity on the youth retreat. Or that you'll talk to 100% of the youth on an individual basis during the youth retreat in order to build relationships.

The method of measuring your objective can be different depending on what the aim actually is. A lot of the time it'll be easy – for example, knowing whether 10 students join a cell group is straightforward enough to measure, as is whether or not 95% of the young people completed a certain activity.

Some measurements can be more subjective though, especially if it relates to how the young people feel about something. Your aim may be that you want the students to grow in self-confidence during the youth retreat. Your specific and measureable objective is that you want 85% of the students to grow in confidence during the retreat. You may feel that this many students have grown in self-confidence judging by their behavior, but that's not a true measurement.

To make this objective more quantifiable, you could ask the youth to complete a questionnaire at the end of the youth retreat telling you how they felt about it. If 85% or more youth agree with the statement, "I have grown in self-confidence at the youth retreat", your aim has been achieved.

**Achievable**

When thinking achievable, don't think easy – hitting a target should take some effort. Company sales targets are set high so that their salespeople will sell as much as they can. Shooters do target practice from far away to perfect their skill. So don't make your objective lame by having it be something that'll be achieved with little to no effort. After all, who has a better feeling of satisfaction – a kicker who makes a 20 yard field goal, or a kicker who makes a 60 yard field goal? (Or for fellow Brits – a footballer that doesn't choke taking a penalty against Germany in the World Cup or Euros).

On the flip side, your youth retreat objective shouldn't be impossible to achieve either. If your aim is to spend one-on-one time with each young person at the youth retreat, that's great. However, if you make it measurable by saying that you'll spend at least one hour talking one-on-one with each youth and you've got 30 young people coming on the retreat, that's almost certainly not going to be achievable unless you're there for a couple of weeks.

Instead, setting the target as a minimum of 10 minutes per youth makes it more achievable, while still requiring effort and proactiveness on your part.

Sometimes the aim might not be one that you set for yourself, but one you set for your helpers. If that's the case, don't forget that what's achievable for you isn't necessarily achievable for other people. Something you find easy might be far more difficult for someone with less experience or different passions to yourself.

For this reason, discuss your aims with your volunteers to involve them in setting objectives. As mentioned above though, don't be afraid to have it require some effort on their part!

**Relevant**

Have you ever worked for an organization that had policies and procedures in place that didn't seem to make sense? Rules which had to be followed that served no purpose? Targets that didn't actually achieve anything? If so, that could be a good sign that those policies, rules and targets weren't relevant to what the organization was aiming for.

Don't let your youth retreat go the same way. When you're creating your objective, think with the end in mind. *What is it that you actually want to achieve on the youth retreat?*

Your objective might be to have at least 90% of the youth take part in a rock-climbing activity. This is specific, measurable and achievable. The thing is, if the purpose of the youth retreat is to enthuse the young people about joining a small group when they get back from the youth retreat, an aim about rock-climbing probably isn't going to be relevant to your ultimate purpose.

Having said that, perhaps the aim of the youth retreat is to help young people overcome their fears and grow in self-confidence. If so, going rock-climbing could be a perfect way of helping to achieve this, making the activity completely relevant to your aim, thereby making the objective relevant as well.

**Time-based**

In order to know that you've achieved an aim, put a deadline on your objective to ensure that it gets completed, otherwise it might just get put off and put off until it's forgotten about. The good thing is, if you're setting an aim for a youth retreat, most of the time it'll have a deadline built in automatically. This is because the objective will generally relate to something you want to achieve at the youth retreat, so the youth retreat is its own deadline.

That might not always be the case though. If your aim is to have a certain number of youth join a small group after the retreat, the youth retreat itself may not be the deadline. Instead, you might choose to set the deadline, in the objective, for the date of the first small group meeting in case you get any last minute sign ups.

To summarize:

- If your objective can address the 5 Ws, this should mean it's **Specific**
- Think in numbers to make your youth retreat **Measurable**
- Your objective should be tough, but **Achievable**
- Knowing what you want to achieve will help your objective be **Relevant**
- Don't put off your objective by making it **Time-based**

A SMART objective may therefore look something like this: "For 75% of the youth to join a small group by 01 December."

One last reminder – *your youth retreat aim doesn't have to be solely related to the actual retreat itself.* It can also be helpful to set aims and objectives throughout the planning process, to ensure that everything that needs doing gets achieved on time, rather than being left to the last minute. These mini-aims could therefore be things like "Book a retreat center by 01 July" and "Provide leadership packs to helpers by 15 November."

## *Action Points:*

- *Choose a theme, aims and objectives early in the retreat planning process*
- *Make objectives SMART*
- *Include youth when choosing a retreat theme*

# 4

## CREATING A BUDGET

This chapter and the next chapter (Choosing a retreat center) could really just be one long chapter. After all, your budget will affect the retreat center you can book, while the cost of the retreat center will affect your budget – a bit of a chicken and egg situation.

There's a lot to cover on both subject areas though, so we've broken them down into two separate chapters. We're starting with many people's most dreaded youth retreat subject – the budget.

There are a lot of different costs that need to be taken into account when calculating a youth retreat budget. We've given a list over the next few pages of many common areas you'll need to budget for – some of these will be applicable to your retreat, while others might not be. Take time to think through each of these areas and try to think of any others applicable to your particular youth retreat, to ensure all possible costs are considered.

## 1) Retreat center

You don't want to book a retreat center that's so expensive that parents can't afford to send their children on the youth retreat, but the cheapest option may result in poor accommodation, a lack of leisure facilities, etc.

*"So how much should I pay for a retreat center?"*

That'll depend on whether you've run a youth retreat in the past or not. If you have, consider the following:

- How much did you charge per student last time?
- Was cost an issue previously?
- Did most (or all) parents find it affordable?

If parents found the cost of the youth retreat affordable last time, keeping the cost to a similar amount would be good, although this might also mean you have a cushion to charge a little more for a better retreat center this year. If cost was an issue previously, this'll give you a good idea of the amount you need to budget for.

Check how much you paid for the retreat center last time, but bear in mind that the cost might have increased since then. Having said that, the retreat center might actually be cheaper this year. If you'd booked the retreat at a busy time of the season last year and this year you're arranging for a different date, you might be able to negotiate a lower price.

If you've never run a youth retreat before or aren't too sure how much to charge for one, knowing how much to budget for a retreat center will inevitably require a little more work. Do some research into retreat centers and get some quotes to find out how much they cost.

Make sure you find out what each retreat center offers for the amount quoted. This means you'll be able to make an accurate cost comparison. For example, one youth retreat center may appear to be significantly cheaper, but that could be because they don't include the cost of meals or the use of leisure facilities.

Many retreat centers charge a flat fee per person attending, although they'll often have a minimum number of attendees to pay for, regardless of how many students are attending the youth retreat. This could end up altering the amount you need to charge per person.

For example, say you're expecting 15 youth to attend, but the retreat center has a minimum booking cost of 20 people. Their fee is $75 per person, so the minimum charge is $1,500 (20 x $75). However, as you're only expecting 15 young people, the flat fee you'd need to charge would be $100 per youth ($1,500 ÷ 15). If you didn't take into account the minimum booking by accident, you'd only charge $1,125 (15 x $75), leaving you with a shortfall of $375.

When working out how many people will be attending, don't forget to include all the leaders and confirm with the retreat center that adults are included in the minimum number of people needed for a booking (they most likely will be). Many centers offer one or more free staff members, based on youth numbers, so check with the retreat center if this is offered.

Alternatively, a youth retreat center might charge a set fee for the use of their facilities, regardless of the number of people attending. For example, the retreat center might charge groups $2,000 for a weekend, so this cost would be split by the number of people attending. If 20 people are expected on the youth retreat, the cost per person would be $100 ($2,000 ÷ 20). If 25 people were attending, the cost per person would be reduced to $80 (2,000 ÷ 25).

**2) Food**
Many youth retreat centers include meals as part of the service they offer but this can vary from site to site, so confirm with them whether or not meals are included. If they are included, check whether there's a surcharge on top of the fee per person you're negotiating, or if meals are already priced into the

quote the retreat center has already provided. If meals aren't included, does the retreat center have kitchen facilities you can use to prepare meals, or would you need to bring along camping stoves?

In the event that you have to prepare the meals yourself, the cost of all the food and drinks for the youth retreat needs to be totaled up. To do this, prepare a menu for the weekend (or however long the youth retreat is for) and list all the ingredients – and quantities – that would be needed. Take the list to your local grocery store and price out how much all the food and drink would come to, then divide it by the number of people due to attend. Don't forget yourself or the volunteers, or you could have some hungry hungry helpers on your hands!

*Tips:*
- *If you or someone you know has membership to Costco, Sam's Club or another wholesaler (in the UK, Makro, Bookers or another cash & carry), take a look at food prices there. As you'll be buying in bulk due to the number of people on the retreat, you might be able to save some money shopping at wholesalers rather than at regular grocery stores.*
- *Even if the retreat center provides three meals a day, check with them whether they also provide snacks and drinks throughout the day. If not, the cost of these will need to be added to the budget.*

- *Are you planning any activities off site? If so, can the center provide packed lunches, or will you need to sort that out yourself? Will you need to bring along bottles of water/other beverages?*

## 3) Volunteers

In addition to yourself, there'll no doubt be other adults there to help you lead the retreat. The cost of these volunteers will therefore need to be taken into account when calculating the total number of people to advise the retreat center, when pricing off-site activities, etc. The next thing to consider is whether the leaders are expected to pay for their own place on the youth retreat, or if their place will be provided free in exchange for their assistance at the retreat.

If the leaders aren't going to be charged, there are a few options as to how this could be covered:

- Their cost could be factored in to what you charge for each young person. Assuming a ratio of one volunteer for every five youth, this would add 20% to the cost for each young person.
- Your church, community organization, charity, etc, could fund their places. Speak to your pastor, treasurer, etc, to see if they have a budget to cover costs such as these.
- Fundraising or grants might be a great way to cover the costs of youth places, thereby

freeing up some of your budget to help cover the cost of volunteers. If you have younger volunteers, you may be able to get funding for their places.

## 4) Speaker

At the youth retreat, will you be having meetings each day? If so, are you planning to bring in an outside speaker, perhaps because they're an expert in the theme you're covering at the retreat?

The cost of their attendance will need to be covered, which will include accommodation, meals and travel. You may also wish to give a donation to the speaker in exchange for their time at the youth retreat, if they're not already charging a certain amount for their services.

## 5) Activities

Some youth retreat centers double as activity centers, meaning there will be plenty for the young people to do, if you want to include those activities as part of the youth retreat. Check with the center though as to whether on-site activities are included in the cost you'd be paying, or if there would be a surcharge (such as for the use of a swimming pool, tennis courts, etc).

Activities don't need to be expensive though – a hike in the woods or a trip to the beach can be very low cost (or even free), but can be excellent bonding opportunities at youth retreats. Other free or low cost activities include treasure hunts and scavenger hunts, water fights, team games or even just free time so the youth can hang out.

When planning the activities, try to think of any possible miscellaneous expenses that might need to be included. If you want to do a water fight, how much would buckets, water balloons and Super Soakers cost? If you're going to the beach, would you have to pay for parking and how much would gas cost to get there and back? Speaking of which.......

**6) Travel & transport**
Where you book the youth retreat and what you're planning to do there will affect whether you need to budget anything for travel and transport.

If parents will be bringing their children to the retreat center, picking them up at the end of the youth retreat and all activities will be done at the retreat center, there shouldn't be any need to budget for travel and transport.

However, if you need to hire a coach, bus, van or minibus to take the youth to and from the retreat center, or will be using one for a trip at some point during the retreat, find out the cost of doing this along with any associated costs such as insurance, gas and parking.

## 7) Resources

If you haven't run a youth retreat before or don't have enough time to also prepare a theme and resources in addition to the rest of the retreat planning, buying youth retreat resources can be very useful in assisting your preparation and the actual leading of the youth retreat. The cost of the resources can then be included in the overall budget.

As time goes on, http://youthworkinit.com/ will be producing resources of this kind for leaders of youth retreats.

## 8) Subsidy

There will often be young people whose families will struggle to afford to send them on events like youth retreats and it would be a shame for them to miss out just because of money issues. Subsidizing the cost of these youth can be done in a few ways:

- Donors or people in your church might be willing to sponsor a place on the youth retreat.
- Your church or community group might have a budget set aside for situations such as these.
- It can be built into the cost of the youth retreat. For example, if 22 young people wanted to come on the youth retreat but two of them couldn't afford it, their cost could be spread over the other 20 people. This would

only add 10% to the cost for each of the other youth – something their families will hopefully be able to afford.

## 9) Prizes

At the youth retreat, are you planning any activities that will require prizes? The prizes may be for games you do at the start of group meetings or a group prize for winning a scavenger hunt.

## 10) Miscellaneous

Each youth retreat is different, so there may be additional costs which aren't included in the above list. For example, if you're doing a youth retreat where you'll be watching a number of movies and the youth will then be discussing issues arising from the films, movie rental will be another cost to include.

When promoting the youth retreat, you may wish to print flyers on brightly colored paper to help get people's attention. The cost of materials like this could be included in the youth retreat budget.

## 11) Buffer

No matter how well you budget for the youth retreat, there will probably be some other unforeseen expenses that will come up. Adding an extra amount as a buffer – about 5% to 10% – will give you a cushion in case anything does crop up. If you don't end up using this buffer, you could either use it to help subsidize places on the youth retreat or keep it set aside and put it towards the next youth retreat.

> *Cross Culture*
> *If your youth retreat is being run through a church, will you be having a worship leader or band at the retreat who aren't your regular volunteers? If so, include the cost of their attendance and possibly a donation.*

~

To help you further with calculating a youth retreat budget, we've produced a free ***Budget Table***. This has spaces for all these expenses and helps you to then calculate the total cost per young person.

When calculating the cost per person, be realistic with the number of young people you expect to come on the youth retreat. If in doubt, err on the side of expecting fewer youth rather than more. Although this will increase the per person cost, if you subsequently have more youth sign up for the retreat than you'd anticipated, the extra funds can be used to subsidize the cost for youth who may not otherwise be able to afford to attend the youth retreat.

If you've not organized a retreat before, or have new youth who haven't been on a retreat you've organized, you probably won't know how much their parents can afford to pay. This makes setting a budget and booking a retreat center a challenge, as you might think the cost of the youth retreat is affordable, only to find out too late that many parents can't afford the cost.

This problem can be avoided though by having parents give feedback on the cost of retreat centers – the largest element of the youth retreat budget. The ***Parent Cost Feedback form*** is a short form to be used once you've got a shortlist of retreat centers to choose from. You briefly outline some of the pros and cons of each center and the estimated cost per person on the table. If possible, try to work out how much the *total* cost would be (taking into account all the factors listed above), rather than just the cost of the retreat centers. This will give parents a much better idea of what's affordable for them.

If you're a youth pastor, there's a good chance a lot of the parents of your youth will go to your church. If that's the case, during a service announce to the parents that you're planning a youth retreat and that you've left a Parent Cost Feedback form at the back of the church (or wherever the most appropriate place is at your church). Advise them that it outlines retreat centers under consideration, the estimated costs and some of the benefits of each one.

Ask the parents to take a look at the form after the service and check a box below the option they would find most affordable. Reassure them that this is anonymous and that you want to gauge what's affordable for most people. Emphasize as well that you want all the young people to come on the youth retreat, so subsidized places are something you'd be able to organize.

If there are a number of parents not at church that week, leave the form where it is and make a similar announcement the following week to try and get as much feedback as possible. By the end of it, you should have a good idea of the budget you have to work with for the youth retreat.

Perhaps you work for a charity or community organization – a similar approach might work for you as well. If the parents of your young people come to your community center, you could ask them to complete the form there.

However, it might be that you don't ever get to meet your young people's parents. If that's the case, consider setting up a free online survey and ask them to complete it, as it would still be anonymous. (There are a number of companies that allow you to create free surveys, one of which is Survey Monkey). If you have the email addresses of the parents, you could then send them a link to the survey. Otherwise, you could send a note home with your young people containing the survey URL.

If you work with low-income families, they may not have internet access at home. You could still get their feedback by sending them a postcard, reply card or envelope with a stamp already attached, meaning it wouldn't cost them anything to reply to you.

An alternative to having parents complete a Parent Cost Feedback form is to have a pre-retreat meeting. Here, you can discuss possible retreat centers, affordable budgets, dates for the youth retreat, etc. This has the added benefit of parents appreciating you taking the time to listen to what they have to say, rather than just going ahead with planning without any feedback from them.

## Action Points:

- *Ensure the budget is thorough and accurate*
- *Budget for subsidized places*
- *Get feedback from parents to ensure you don't make the retreat unaffordable for most of them*

# 5

# CHOOSING A RETREAT CENTER

As mentioned at the beginning of the last chapter, creating a budget and choosing a retreat center are intertwined, as both factors impact on each other. The last chapter focused on the cost of retreat centers, while this chapter will focus on all the other aspects of booking a retreat center.

Although we refer to retreat centers throughout this chapter, there are many other possible venues you may wish to consider based on your group size, age, budget and desired skills or outcomes (see Chapter 3). Here are a few possible options to help you with your research:

- Dedicated retreat center
- Activity center
- Hotel
- Youth camp
- Cottage
- Vacation rental homes (beach or mountain)
- Church
- Community center/rec center

The retreat center you book can have a huge effect on the tone of the retreat, along with what activities you're able to do. It's therefore best to book a retreat center about 6 – 12 months before you're planning on holding the youth retreat.

## 6 – 12 months? Seriously?!?!

We're afraid so! Retreat centers can get booked up quickly, especially during popular times of the year, so if you wait closer to the time it could mean that there are no suitable retreat centers available. Many centers offer tiered pricing based on how far in advance you book, meaning you can run the retreat on a smaller budget. For example, a center might charge $200 per youth if you book 9 – 12 months in advance, while the price increases to $250 six months before.

If you're organizing a youth retreat then, chances are that you need to start looking for a retreat center now, regardless of when it's going to be. However, your organization might create activity calendars up to a year in advance, so the earlier you can find and book a retreat center, the more helpful it will be for scheduling purposes.

You have lots of possible venues and a date, so how do you find retreat centers? Here are a few suggestions:

## Personal experiences

If you've visited a retreat center before and enjoyed your time there, that's a good place to start.

## Other people's experiences

Talk to youth pastors, youth workers, friends, family, pastors, work colleagues – anyone you can think of! Does your workplace ever organize team-building days or weekends? If they do, speak to the person who plans them in case there are any retreat centers they can recommend for your youth retreat.

Has your church or organization held other retreats in the past (e.g. men's, women's, marriage, etc)? If so, were the retreat centers popular with those who attended the retreat, or did they encounter any problems that you should consider?

Don't forget social networks too – ask people on Twitter, Facebook, Google+, etc if they've got any recommendations. On Twitter, try using hashtags like #ywchat to help people find your question.

## Search online

Do searches for terms like "retreat center", "activity center", "retreats", "youth retreats", etc. Also do these searches followed by your city or state to ensure you get retreat center results that are more local to you. If you live close to the border of another state, try doing a search for there too, in case there's a retreat center still fairly close by.

Keep an eye on the ads on the right hand side of search engines as well – you may find retreat centers advertising themselves there.

Once you've found some retreat centers, do searches for the names of the retreat centers, followed by "review". This might bring up some reviews of the retreat center from people who have actually been there before and alert you to any problems they had.

**Yellow Pages**
Take a look in your local Yellow Pages, as you may find some retreat centers in there.

Once you've done some researching, you'll hopefully have found a number of possible centers for the youth retreat. Make a list of these, along with a note of their website address if you found them online (or bookmark them in your browser).

~

One important factor to take into account when booking a retreat center is its location. On the one hand, you might not want the youth retreat to be so far away that it takes hours of driving in order to get to the retreat center. On the other hand, it'll probably more fun for the youth if it's not just around the corner from where they live – unfamiliar surroundings create a far greater sense of adventure on a youth retreat.

Something else to consider is how the youth will be getting to the retreat center. Are parents going to be asked to drive their children to the center and collect them at the end of the retreat, or will they all drop off and pick up their children at a set location – perhaps your church or community center – for you to then transport the youth to the retreat center?

If the parents are expected to drive their children to the youth retreat, encourage them to car pool. That way, one family could take them and the other family could pick them up at the end of the retreat.

~

Youth retreats (along with most other retreats) tend to be held at retreat centers that are in secluded areas. There's no reason why that always has to be the case though. One of the main purposes of a retreat is to disconnect from everyday life in order to focus on something else – yourself, God, your marriage or any number of other things. If you live in a rural area, holding your youth retreat in an urban area might actually be more retreat-like than if you were to hold it in the countryside at a nearby location. This might also put you closer to additional activities for your retreat, or possible community service opportunities.

On the flip-side, perhaps you work for a church or community organization in an inner-city area with low-income families. Unless you have donors who contribute towards the cost of the youth retreat, your budget will probably be quite low and might mean holding the retreat outside of the city is too costly. If that's the case, one solution would be to have the youth sleep at your church or community center, but take them to a park each day so that they still feel like they're out of the city. You could not only do activities all day in the park, but you could also make lunch each day a picnic – something the youth may not have experienced before.

Retreat centers in rural locations can be perfect though if you're wanting to do outdoor activities. There will usually be opportunities for hiking, outdoor games, etc, as well as picturesque views and quiet surroundings.

Urban locations can be better if there are certain off-site activities you want to do or if your youth that live in a rural community could do with a taste of the big city, while a beach location where they can see the ocean will be exhilarating for inland youth. It all depends on what you're wanting to achieve with the youth retreat, which goes back to your youth retreat aims.

Your youth retreat aim and theme will also come in handy when evaluating a retreat center's facilities. For example:

- "Sport" theme – a center with basketball courts, a running track, swimming pool, etc, will be useful.
- "Nature" theme – a retreat in a forest, in the mountains or at the beach will lend itself well to teaching about this subject.
- "Team-building" aim – a retreat center that has lots of activities where the young people have to work as a team will reinforce your message.
- "Finding your way in life" theme – a center with lots of hiking opportunities could be used to improve map-reading skills and link in with this.

*Cross Culture*
*Alternative versions might be a "Creation" theme or "Following God's Directions" theme, while a team-building aim could link in with 1 Corinthians 12: 12-31 – one body, many parts.*

Doing all this should give you a shortlist of retreat centers. To help you whittle the list down, compile a list of questions to ask the retreat centers that could have an impact on how you run the youth retreat.

The questions will differ depending on what you have planned, but here is a list of different questions to consider that might prompt some other areas for you to enquire about:

**1) Is there a minimum number of young people needed in order to book the facility?**
Be realistic – are you likely to have that many people coming on the retreat, as the retreat center will still require payment for that minimum number, regardless of how many youth end up attending.

**2) Are there additional charges for using facilities on site?**
If there's a pool, do you have to pay extra to have a lifeguard on duty? If there are tennis courts, do you have to pay extra for tennis rackets?

**3) Can you have a camp fire?**
If so, do you need to collect firewood or can the center provide that? Even if the center can provide it, searching for firewood is a great team-building opportunity on the youth retreat.

**4) Are you going to be the only group at the retreat center?**
At a large retreat center, you might find that other groups are there at the same time as you. Find out if this will impact on you being able to use any of the facilities like the swimming pool, meeting room, etc.

## 5) Are there TV & DVD facilities if you need them?

Also check if these are always available, or if they have to be booked.

## 6) Is there a projector available for presentations?

Check on the projector's location as well, (e.g. fixed to the ceiling, stand-alone, etc) as this may affect the layout of the meeting room.

## 7) Is bedding provided?

Most retreat centers will provide bedding, but a budget retreat center might expect you to bring sleeping bags instead.

## 8) Is toilet paper included?

OK, we know this is a weird question. But some retreat centers ask that you bring everything you might need, so it would be a shame to get there and find that you're TP free!

## 9) Are towels provided?

Again, this is something else you might expect will be provided, but many retreat centers will ask you to bring your own towels.

## 10) What time can we arrive and what time do we have to leave?

A retreat center might have a policy of requiring you to leave the site at midday on the final day of your booking. This could therefore impact on your plans if you didn't want to leave until later in the day.

## 11) Is the cost of meals included?
Also, are snacks included or do you have to bring them yourself? Otherwise, are there vending machines?

## 12) What indoor facilities are there?
If adverse weather meant that you couldn't do any outdoor activities or games, does the youth retreat center have adequate indoor facilities to keep young people entertained?

When asking all these questions, make a note of who you spoke to at the retreat center and on what date. Asking these questions via email is even better, as you've then got a written record from the retreat center to revert back to in the event of any problems regarding what was advised.

~

These questions should help you narrow down the list of possible retreat centers. Now that you've got a shorter list, try to visit the retreat centers if you can. This will give you a much better idea of what to expect and help you plan the youth retreat accordingly. You might also find out the reason why a retreat center doesn't have any photos of their "facilities" on their website!

This stage is also a good time to use the Parent Cost Feedback form to get input on how much families can afford in order to send their children on the youth retreat – see the previous chapter for a recap on this.

If you've now done thorough research into possible retreat centers, received feedback from parents and visited the retreat center(s), you'll hopefully have a good idea of which retreat center you want to book. Here are 5 tips for what to do when booking the retreat center:

## 1) Contract
Once you've chosen a retreat center, reserve it as soon as you can. The best youth retreat centers get booked early, so don't miss out on your ideal location. As mentioned previously, it's best to try booking the retreat center at least 6 months in advance. Although this may seem quite early, it means you'll have a much better selection of sites to choose from for your youth retreat, rather than having to choose a mediocre one at the last minute simply because it's the only one available.

## 2) Commit
Retreat centers often require a deposit when booking. Speak to the person in charge of finances at your church, charity or community organization in advance to ensure that it won't be a problem paying this before you've received payment from parents.

## 3) Confirm

When booking the youth retreat center, confirm with them any specifics such as the minimum number of students attending, whether meals are included, etc, and ask for it in writing – either by email or letter. This will help ensure there's no miscommunication or false expectations regarding these areas, helping the planning of the youth retreat to go more smoothly.

## 4) Communicate

If you're in charge of the youth retreat but have delegated the booking of the retreat center to somebody else, make sure you check that this person has actually made the reservation. This may sound obvious, but mix-ups can happen! It would be horrible to turn up and find out the other person had thought you'd been the one who was supposed to book the retreat center.

## 5) Calculate

It might be that through all your research, there just aren't any affordable retreat centers. If you're a youth pastor, does your church have adequate facilities for housing students over a weekend – showers, a kitchen, etc? If so, consider holding the youth retreat there. It's not as ideal as being able to take the youth away to a retreat center, but they can still benefit greatly from the youth retreat.

Maybe you work for a charity or community group that has a limited budget. Does your organization have a community center you could use for the youth retreat? If not, is there a nearby church or another community group which has facilities you could use for a weekend? The young people will still get to be away from home for a couple of nights, spend the weekend with friends and make new friends, so don't allow the lack of an affordable retreat center prevent you from organizing a youth retreat.

### *Action Points:*

- *If possible, pick a retreat center that complements your theme*
- *Keep records of communication with the retreat center*
- *Be thorough when researching what each retreat center offers*

# 6

## PROMOTING YOUR YOUTH RETREAT

There are many ways to drive up interest in a youth retreat and ensure that as many young people as possible are motivated into signing up. Although not exhaustive, using these ideas should help get your youth group enthused about the retreat.

**Create a flyer**
A good method of promoting the retreat is to enlist the help of some of your creative and artsy students to create a flyer. Having some of the young people involved with creating a flyer has a few benefits:

- It should mean the flyer is more appealing to youth
- It'll get the students who designed it more involved in the youth retreat and therefore more likely to attend
- These students will be more passionate about the youth retreat and so will be more vocal with getting their friends to sign up as well

The flyer doesn't need a huge amount of information, but make sure you include the following:

- Where the youth retreat center is
- The dates it's being held, along with the start and end times
- How much the youth retreat will cost
- What you'll be doing there in terms of the theme
- What you'll be doing there in terms of activities. You don't need to go into great detail with this if you don't have all the activities planned yet – even just mention you'll be doing games, having a camp fire, etc.
- Contact information for the person that will be taking registrations and payment for the youth retreat

Generally, A5 sized paper (half-sheet sized) is best for flyers – this is 210mm x 148mm (or 8 & ¼ x 5 & ⅞ inches). Using colored paper can be a great way of drawing attention to the flyer unless the design is already colorful and vibrant, in which case regular white paper might be more appropriate.

The next thing to decide is how many flyers you need to print out. If you're only wanting the young people in your youth group to attend, you'll obviously only need to print a limited supply of flyers; perhaps two per youth – one for each young person and one for them to give to their parents.

However, if you're planning on opening up the youth retreat to your youth group's friends, then you'll need to print far more flyers. Encourage your young people to take plenty of them to hand out to their friends. If the youth retreat is open to all the young people in your community, get some of the youth to help you put flyers in mailboxes in the neighborhood, in store windows, etc.

**Announce the retreat to the youth**
Don't do this until you've booked the retreat center, as it will mean you have more information to be able to give them.

When letting the youth know about the retreat, you'll want to announce it in a different way to the approach taken with their parents. Parents will want to know about some of the specifics and practical points (e.g. dates, cost, etc), whereas the young people will want to know more about what they'd be doing and why they should want to come.

Even if everything isn't fully planned out yet, make sure you've got enough information to get them excited about the retreat at this early stage. If the retreat center has some great facilities (e.g. swimming pool, assault course, etc), see if you can get some photos to show the youth. If you think the theme will have particular resonance with your group of young people, emphasize that.

Encourage them to invite their friends (if the retreat is open to them) and give them some flyers to pass out to their friends. Also, get the youth to give their parents a copy of the flyer. In addition to the flyer, provide a registration form (see the next chapter for more details on that).

**Announce the retreat to parents**
Young people aren't always great about remembering to tell their parents about events or passing on information sheets you've asked them to give to their parents. Therefore, once you've booked the retreat center, take the opportunity to advise the parents about the youth retreat. The way you do this will differ depending on the type of organization you work for.

If the retreat is being run through a church, the best opportunity to announce the retreat to parents will probably be during a service. If you work for a charity or community organization, sending the information to parents by mail will probably be a better option, unless you see their parents each week (perhaps when they drop off or pick up their children).

A copy of the flyer and registration form should be given to all the parents, along with an information letter if you're sending them by mail.

**Remind youth each week about the event**

Don't spend too long each time talking about it, but reminding the young people about the youth retreat each week will help maintain excitement and interest. Start doing this 2 – 3 weeks leading up to registration and payment deadlines and again 2 – 3 weeks before the actual retreat.

**Use social media**

- **Create a Facebook event** and invite all the youth who are on Facebook. You can upload photos of the retreat center, photos and videos from previous youth retreats to remind them of the fun they had last time, etc. You can then update them with more information as time goes on, such as directions to get to the site, the youth retreat schedule, etc. This is also a good opportunity for the young people to invite their friends and give them an idea of how much fun it will be.
- **Set up a Twitter account** for the youth retreat and encourage your youth who are on Twitter to follow it. Have them retweet the retreat!
- **Set up a website for the youth retreat.** Even if you can set up a website yourself, it's a good idea to ask some of the tech-savvy or creative youth in your group to help design the site. This will increase their interest in the youth retreat and encourage them to

promote the site with their friends. Parents can also check the site if they want more information about the retreat. If there aren't any youth that can help design the site, you may find one of our next books useful – How to create a free youth group website.

## Speak to every young person individually

Ask each member of your youth group individually if they'll be coming to the retreat. Emphasize to them how much you want them there – if they weren't planning on coming before, having an adult tell them how much they'd love to have them be part of the retreat can make a real difference. This personal touch will not only help encourage them to come to the retreat, but will also help build a more personal relationship with the young person, as they'll feel more cared for as an individual.

If you have a large youth group that makes it hard to speak to every young person, at least make sure that other youth leaders have spoken to every young person.

## Film a video

Play the video during your youth group about a month before the retreat, as well as to their parents if you get an opportunity (like at a pre-retreat parent meeting).

*Cross Culture*

*A great opportunity would be during a church service.*

As with the flyers, ask some of your more creative students to help you with this and make the video as entertaining as possible.

The video could:

- Revolve around the theme of the retreat
- Be done in the form of a news report, with students taking leading roles as reporters
- Have footage of the retreat center
- Have footage of previous youth retreats

**Don't let cost be an issue**

Regardless of how low you've tried to keep the cost of the youth retreat, there will probably be some parents who can't afford the full cost of the retreat. Ensure both parents and young people know that you want all the youth to be able to attend the youth retreat, regardless of cost.

Encourage them to contact you (or the person dealing with the registration) to discuss the possibility of subsidizing the youth retreat for those students. Giving them an email address might help with this, as they may be more willing to discuss this via email than face-to-face.

Also, speak to your pastor, treasurer, etc, beforehand to organize some funds to help parents send their children on the retreat, if subsidized places haven't already been built into the cost of the youth retreat.

*Tips:*

- *As you may have noticed, we think youth participation is important, not just in youth retreat planning but in all areas of your youth work. The more you can get the youth involved in promoting the retreat, the better. Young people are more likely to be influenced by their peers encouraging them to join the retreat than if their parents do.*
- *When making a video to promote the youth retreat, try to film it on location at the retreat center, providing it's not too far away and the center will allow it. This will have many benefits – you'll get a great opportunity to build a relationship with the youth helping with the video, they'll get to see the retreat center and tell their friends about how good it is, plus youth and parents will be able to see some video footage of the facilities.*

*Action Points:*

- *Use as many methods of promotion as possible – traditional, online, social media, etc*
- *Encourage youth to promote the retreat*

# 7

# REGISTRATION PROCESS

About 3 – 6 months before the retreat, it's time to start the registration process, although don't do this until you've booked the retreat center. Registration forms can be handed out to both youth and parents, with extra copies left at the back of your church, in the lobby of your community center, etc. in case anybody misplaces theirs.

A sample **_Registration Form_** is another free template you get with this book – see the introduction for details on how to get this.

The registration form will need certain information clearly stated in order for youth and parents to know exactly what they're signing up to. Some information that should definitely be included:

- The dates of the retreat
- Where it's being held
- The cost
- Whether a non-refundable deposit fee is required (typically about 10-20%)
- Who checks should be made payable to

- Name and contact details of the person dealing with registrations
- The date you need their reply (and deposit if applicable) by
- The date the balance will be due

At the bottom of the form, it's worth having a cut-off section for parents to complete in order to advise whether or not their child(ren) will be attending the event. Have the cut-off section request the deposit fee at the same time as they return the slip to the person dealing with the registrations.

As you start to receive replies as to who will or won't be attending, create a spreadsheet listing all those you've heard from and those who are yet to reply. This will facilitate with keeping track of the numbers that are due to come on the retreat.

You might receive replies confirming some young people will be attending but the deposit won't be included at the time. Keep track of these cases in an extra column on the spreadsheet to ensure that you know who you still require deposits from. If somebody else is dealing with the registration forms, keep in close contact with them so that you know where you are with numbers attending.

If you've not received many replies after a couple of weeks, remind the parents about the youth retreat again – either by making an announcement in a church service, a note mailed to them, etc. Also encourage the youth in your group to sign up as soon as possible. The sooner you have an idea of how many youth will be attending, the easier it will be to plan activities for the youth retreat, organize transport to the retreat center, etc.

Once you've started to receive registration forms for the youth retreat, have parents or guardians complete a ***Parental Consent Form (PCF)***. These forms should be returned before the retreat – advise the parents that their child won't be able to attend the youth retreat unless one of these forms has been completed and returned.

It's best to provide these forms for completion no more than one month before the youth retreat. Although on the one hand it would make sense to include the PCF with the registration form, having the PCF completed closer to the date of the youth retreat will help ensure that the medical information is up-to-date. If the form had been completed a few months earlier, it might leave off that Billy has a peanut allergy that they only found out about a few weeks later.

The Parental Consent Form should request a lot of important information about the youth who will be attending the retreat, including the following:

- Name of the child
- Date of birth
- Address & phone number
- Parent's/guardian's names and phone numbers
- Other emergency contact name and phone number
- Allergies
- Any medication being taken, including instructions (EpiPens, inhalers, etc)
- Any other important health information (learning difficulties, Asperger's syndrome, etc)
- Basic medical care consent (e.g. OTC medications such as ibuprofen or Midol for headaches, female cramping, etc)
- Dietary requirements (e.g. vegetarian, lactose intolerant, etc)
- Medical insurance information
- Disclaimer and consent
- Parent's signature

Put one person in charge of collecting the PCFs and make sure that all of the forms are brought to the youth retreat. In the event of a medical emergency, you would then be able to show the hospital that you have the authorization to make any necessary decisions, as well as providing medics with details of any relevant allergies, medication, etc.

If any of the youth due to come on the youth retreat have a significant health issue, advise all of the volunteers who will be at the retreat. This is so that all of the leadership team can be aware of anything that they should be looking out for. For example, one of the students may suffer from epilepsy, so it's important that all of the adults know this, especially if you'll be doing activities like swimming or hiking in the mountains.

If any of the youth suffer from a medical condition that you don't know anything about, talk to their parents about it. They should be happy to give you any information you need, seeing as their child's health is involved. This will also reassure their parents about any concerns they may have, as it shows that you're being proactive about safety.

A week or two before the final cut-off date for registration, have another big push to get as many young people signed up as possible. Chat to parents of students who have either said they can't attend or who haven't replied yet – it might be that they're concerned about the cost. At this late stage, you may have exceeded the numbers you were expecting to come on the retreat, so you might be able to give a larger subsidy, or perhaps offer some more free places.

*Tips:*

- *If you're likely to misplace the slips of paper parents return from the registration form, use a scanner at your organization or at home to make a copy that's saved to your computer. If you scan copies of the PCF as well, remember to take either the originals or printed off copies with you to the retreat.*
- *Consider providing parents with 24 hour contact details for the relevant person in your organization in the event of an emergency.*
- *Additional information you may wish to include on your registration form includes the times the retreat will begin and end, the theme of the youth retreat and any special activities the young people will be doing.*
- *When you receive deposits, give the parents a receipt. Receipt books can be purchased cheaply from Staples, Walmart, dollar stores, etc. If possible, give the receipt directly to the parents rather than to their child, in case the young person forgets to pass it on.*
- *Have a supply of Parental Consent Forms on hand the day of the retreat. This means that if a parent hasn't completed a form yet for their child, they can do so when dropping them off.*
- *Provide the young people with a checklist of things to bring to the retreat you think they might need, such as a flashlight, pen & paper, spending money if doing an off-site visit, etc.*

## *Action Points:*

- *Be organized when registering youth*
- *Get thorough information on consent forms*

# 8

# INVOLVING YOUTH IN RETREAT PLANNING

In the second chapter, we looked at volunteers and other people that could help you plan a youth retreat, even if they didn't want to be involved with the actual youth work side of things. There's another demographic of people that can help you plan a youth retreat and they have a vested interest in making sure the youth retreat is interesting – youth themselves.

At Youth Workin' It, we're big fans of youth participation. Giving young people an opportunity to influence the work you do with them can seem like an alien concept at first, but it provides so many benefits. It gives them some level of ownership over your youth programs, meaning they will be more likely to help it succeed. It creates humility in us as youth workers by forcing us to give up some of our power and passing the influence to others. It also gives young people an opportunity to be rational decision-makers as they grow up and become young adults, as well as giving them a chance to shine, improving their self-worth.

This doesn't mean that you give 14 year olds unrestricted control of a $5,000 youth retreat budget or put them in charge of doing risk assessments. There are many areas though that you can involve youth in when it comes to retreat planning. This will get the youth even more excited about the retreat, which will hopefully be contagious and will result in this enthusiasm spreading to their friends.

**Creating a youth retreat website**
We've touched on creating a website for the youth retreat earlier in the book. Even if you have the skills to set up a website yourself, why not give one or two of the techie young people an opportunity to help you put the website together. Alternatively, teach a young person that needs some one-to-one time if you know how to design websites, or connect them with a caring mentor that does.

**Filming and editing videos**
Many youth groups contain a budding filmmaker or two, so why not give them an opportunity to gain more experience and create something their friends will really connect with. If you have video footage from previous youth retreats, they can edit the best bits together in a video montage to help promote this year's youth retreat. Once you've booked the retreat center, you could take them on a visit there

to get some footage of the facilities. This will be a great bonding opportunity, especially if you take your volunteers along at the same time.

This would also work well as a media project for your youth programs.

**Graphic design**
I don't know about you, but I'm not at all artsy (I being Stephen – Shae's the better creative half). If I create a flyer to promote a youth retreat, it doesn't really catch the eye.

I mentioned in the last point that many youth groups contain a budding filmmaker – most groups will also contain at least one creative, artsy student. Make the most of their gifting and have them help you design a flyer. Do this even if you're artsy yourself and love to design, as it'll mean so much to the youth to be given the responsibility to create something like this.

**Picking a youth retreat theme**
This is something else we've touched on previously, but if you want to pick a youth retreat theme that's relevant to the lives of your youth, who are better placed to know what this would be than the students themselves?

Granted, young people can easily go off-topic and end up spending a whole session coming up with 173 different themes ranging from the Biebs (girls) to bodily functions (boys). Good facilitation of the discussion should help with this, or you could provide a shortlist of possible youth retreat themes to pick from (see Chapter 3 for more details on this).

## Activities
Depending on the retreat center you book, there might be all kinds of activities available for you to organize, but you may not have time to do all of them on the youth retreat. Get your youth participating in the retreat planning by giving them a list of possible activities and asking them to pick their favorite one or two. You can then pick the most popular activities to do at the youth retreat.

## Promotion
When trying to spread the word about the youth retreat, no one will reach other young people like young people themselves. So put them in charge of promoting the retreat – through flyers, email, Facebook, Twitter, word of mouth, etc. If they're enthusiastic about the youth retreat, they're far more likely to invite other friends.

## Menu and food shopping
If your retreat center doesn't provide meals, you'll need to organize them yourself. Include your young people in putting together a menu for the youth retreat, although there's a good chance this will result in BANANAS (Burgers And Nuggets, Avoid Nutrients And Salad).

This will also mean food shopping. It might sound weird, but going shopping at a grocery store is a great bonding opportunity for you and your young people – pick a few though, not fifty! Keep a close eye on all the Kit-Kats being put in the shopping cart as well.

## Fundraising

If your youth retreat is going to be too expensive for some young people, fundraising is a great way to provide subsidized (or free) places. Get your youth involved in fundraising – for some ideas, you can check out our blog posts providing youth fundraising ideas at http://youthworkinit.com/category/youth-fundraiser/

Alternatively, you could ask for sponsorship from businesses or goods in kind.

## *Action Point:*

- *If you're going to organize something for the retreat, ask yourself "Is this something the youth could help with?"*

# 9

# RISK ASSESSMENTS

When you're responsible for taking youth away to another location for a retreat, it's important to do what you can to ensure that they're kept safe. The best way of doing this is to perform a risk assessment. A risk assessment is used as a method of identifying potential hazards and then evaluating if there's anything that can be done to either prevent or reduce the risk of an accident occurring.

**Identify the hazard**
As the youth retreat is probably being held somewhere fairly (or completely) unfamiliar to you, it can be hard to know what things might cause harm there. In the previous chapters, we've suggested visiting the retreat center. If you do visit it, take that opportunity to identify any potential hazards. Try to involve your volunteers in this process – it will mean that they're more aware of the hazards, plus they may identify hazards that you miss. The retreat center isn't the only place to identify hazards – if you're planning any off-site activities, there might be risks involved there too.

The kinds of potential hazards to look out for include:

- Swimming pools
- Propane tanks
- Hiking paths
- Bonfires
- Electricity
- Lighting (or lack of it)
- Fire exits
- Heatstroke or hypothermia (depending on the time of the year)

**Who might be harmed?**
Many hazards will affect everyone on the camp, such as electricity, bonfires, etc. However, it may be that some people will be more susceptible to risks than others. Take extra care when considering people (whether youth or adults) who have particular needs. Some of the students may not be very good at swimming, a volunteer may have poor eyesight or a young person might be on crutches or in a wheelchair. These factors will affect their susceptibility to hazards.

Also be aware of the behavior of the students, as that might affect their potential risk of hazards. We know of one camp where a young person would sneak off to have a cigarette and chose to hide behind where the propane gas tank was fenced off. He would then throw the cigarette stubs over the fence, as he wasn't aware that the propane gas tank was housed in there. Thankfully this was discovered before anything bad happened, but it highlights how unexpected hazards can be!

**Evaluate risks and take appropriate precautions**
Now that you've identified the hazards, you need to ask yourself what the likelihood is of a hazard occurring. If you're going hiking in bad weather, you may deem the risk to be high. Going swimming in a pool with two trained lifeguards will likely be regarded as a lower risk. The likelihood of an incident occurring will depend on a number of factors, whether that be the weather, the age of your youth, the layout of the retreat center, etc.

Once you've considered the chances of a hazard occurring, identify whether you can avoid the hazard completely, or if there's anything that can be done to reduce the risk of it happening. There are a number of ways this can be done:

- **Prevent access** – an unattended swimming pool could prove risky if youth are able to access it at any time. However, if the pool is inside, can the door be locked to ensure no students can enter the pool area unless there's a lifeguard on duty?
- **Avoid the risk** – if there's a propane tank on site, organize any activities away from it, especially things like bonfires, sports, etc.

- **Choose a less risky option** – if there's a dangerous hiking path, choose a different route.
- **Provide protective equipment** – if some of your students aren't good swimmers, provide floatation devices if you go swimming.
- **Organization** – if you're having a bonfire, rather than asking students to grab a chair and sit around the bonfire, have the chairs already in place. This will help ensure they sit a safe distance from the fire.
- **Knowledge** – when you first get to the retreat center, make sure the youth are aware of the fire exits and where to meet in the event of a fire
- **First aid** – have a first aid kit on hand in case accidents do happen.
- **Communication** – if you're going on a hike, carry your cell phone with you in case someone is hurt and an ambulance needs to be called.

**Record the hazards and risks and implement precautions**

*\*\*This next section is best read with the **Risk Assessment** template\*\**

After identifying all the potential hazards and risks, write down the results of what you've found so that you have a record. This will serve as a good reference point when organizing activities and will prove that safety on the retreat was considered in the event of an accident actually happening.

One way of recording hazards and risks is to rate them on a scale of severity and likelihood. The severity scale ranges from Negligible (1) to Very Severe (5), whereas the likelihood ranges from Very Unlikely (1) to Almost Certain (5).

Depending on your preference, you can choose to use either the colored scale or the numerical scale (whereby you multiply the two numbers together) in order to assess the overall risk for each activity or location.

Using the template and example we've provided, if a hazard falls within the yellow or red risk levels, or has an overall risk rating of eight and above, it's worth considering whether it can be avoided completely, or whether anything can be done to lessen the potential harm or likelihood of it happening.

While identifying hazards and risk levels are important, setting out a plan to address hazards and lower the level of risk is the most critical part of the risk assessment process. To do this, look at each hazard individually and determine what action (if any) can be taken to reduce the likelihood or severity of the activity or location – these are called control measures.

For example, if you're going to be using a swimming pool, potential hazards might include drowning, slip and fall accidents, horseplay/flips in water and sunburn/dehydration (if the pool is outside). In this example, you might list the following control measures:

- **Drowning** – swimming listed on parental consent form (including water depth); provision of floatation devices and/or life preservers; lifeguard on duty; first aider present
- **Slip and fall accidents** – pre-swimming safety talk; written rules on display; appropriate adult:youth ratio for supervision and correction
- **Horseplay/flips in water** – pre-swimming safety talk; written rules on display; appropriate adult:youth ratio for supervision and correction
- **Sunburn/dehydration** – safety talk about signs of sunburn and dehydration; sunscreen included on youth packing list; first aiders to have sunscreen and water available; limit swimming session time

n.b. This isn't an exhaustive list of potential hazards or control measures – the responsibility falls on you, your team, your organization and/or the retreat center to identify and address all potential hazards and risks.

## Communicate

If there are risks that the adults or youth should be made aware of, make sure that this is well communicated. With the adults, the primary risks could be listed in a leadership pack you provide before the retreat. For the youth, the risks they should be aware of (such as location of fire exits) could be covered during the first group meeting.

## Review the assessment

Just before the retreat, review the risk assessment again – if possible, get to the retreat center early in order to conduct the review. Check whether any of the hazards have changed or if there are any new hazards. Other factors may have changed too – perhaps the weather is worse than you were anticipating so hikes would be more risky, or the retreat center is no longer able to provide a lifeguard for the swimming pool.

Update the assessment as necessary and make the adults (and youth if applicable) on the retreat aware of any appropriate changes. Also ensure that everybody at the retreat is advised of the procedure in the event of a fire – communicate this as early as possible on the retreat.

*Action Points:*

- *Check if the retreat center has completed risk assessments*
- *Perform your own assessments for activities that aren't on a retreat center risk assessment*
- *Always be looking for ways to improve safety*

# 10

## MEETINGS

If your youth retreat is being run through a church, the main meetings are one of the best opportunities to be able to pour into the spiritual lives of the youth. This is therefore one of the areas it's best to focus a lot of attention on when it comes to preparation for the retreat.

The first thing to consider is who will be speaking at the youth retreat. If you're a youth pastor there's a good chance that this responsibility will fall to you, but this doesn't have to be the case. If there's somebody else who has more expertise in the theme of your retreat, you could try to book them as a guest speaker. One benefit of this is that you're freed up to focus on other areas of the retreat. However, it might mean that you would wish to provide a donation for their services on the retreat, increasing the cost of the retreat.

If you do book a guest speaker, make sure they're clear on what you want to cover as the theme. If you advise them that the theme is 'Love', they may prepare their talks relating to teenage love and relationships, whereas you had wanted them to talk about God's love.

Be specific and keep in contact with them as they prepare the talks. Ask them for an overview of what they'll be covering in each meeting – not only will it mean that you'll both be on the same page as to what they'll be talking about, it will also help you with the rest of the preparation. The subject of the talk could affect the choice of worship songs, what games are played in the meetings, discussions after the meeting, devotions and more.

Another option is to have different volunteers prepare talks for the meetings. Again, this may be of benefit as it allows you to focus on other areas of the retreat. One potential drawback with having a number of people giving talks is that you may not get quite as much consistency with the theme of your retreat as you would from just one person preparing the talks.

If you decide to have a number of different people speak at the meetings, let them know at least a month in advance the subject that you would like them to talk about, as this will give them plenty of time to prepare. Keep in contact with all the people due to speak and ask them for an overview of what they will be covering. This will ensure that not only are they definitely covering the topic you've given them, but it will also help identify whether two people look like they're going to be covering the same area.

For example, if your theme is 'Faith', you may have more than one person who plans to talk about Joshua and the walls of Jericho. If you don't know about this in advance, you may have one of the volunteers finding out at a morning meeting that someone else has used that story, giving them only a few hours until the evening meeting to change their talk so that they can cover a different story from the Bible.

In the event that it's not just you talking at the meetings – whether that's due to having a guest speaker or having volunteers speaking –find out if there's anything they need for what they have planned. The room may need to be set up differently, they may need a laptop and projector or a TV and DVD player, etc.

Having good communication in the run-up to the youth retreat will reduce the number of problems you encounter. It will also instill confidence in the guest speaker or volunteers that the retreat will be well organized and that they won't have to worry about things not being right by the time it's too late to actually change anything.

The way you order the main meetings is completely up to you – there's no right or wrong way. There can be many different elements you may wish to incorporate into the meetings and the ones you use may differ from meeting to meeting. Here are some ideas of things to include:

**Teaching session**
The talk will probably be the primary way of getting across the teaching of your theme during the retreat. It provides a great opportunity to pour truth into their lives, in an environment that makes them more likely to stop and consider what you have to say.

When speaking, it shouldn't last much more than 30 minutes, as the youths' attention will start to wander. It's therefore worth incorporating other elements into the talks to help with short attention spans:

**Humor**
This is very effective in maintaining focus on your message. If you can get the young people to laugh, your credibility with them will rise and they'll be more likely to listen to what else you have to say. Your whole talk shouldn't just be one punchline after another, but well-placed humor will help keep their interest on the other important points you're making.

**Video**
If you're concerned that the youth on your retreat will have a hard time focusing on you talking for a

long time, consider incorporating a video into your talk. The video might only be a few minutes long, but it could provide a useful way of illustrating a point which doesn't involve you having to verbalize it. The video may be a movie clip, some kind of random (but related) Youtube video or even footage you've filmed yourself.

**Include others**
Another way to avoid making the youth listen to only you for half an hour, is to include other people. One option would be to ask a young person or adult to share a testimony relating to the subject of what you're speaking about that day. A testimony from a young person is particularly useful, as it can help show the other youth how this has particular relevance in their lives.

One quick point on all this though: anything you incorporate into your talk should be *relevant* to your theme. It's all very well including a funny video, but if it doesn't relate to the theme it'll only serve to confuse your group.

Likewise, testimonies can play an important role in personally relating the theme to the lives of the youth. However, if the testimony that's shared doesn't really relate to the theme of your talk, it's questionable as to whether it serves its purpose. If you ask somebody to share a testimony, make the theme clear to them and when they've had a chance to prepare their testimony, ask them to share it with you. This will not only help ensure that it's relevant to your talk, but it will help you to plan what to say after their testimony, directly linking it back to the theme again.

When giving the talk, be passionate. Retreats are an amazing opportunity to enthuse young people about your theme, but they'll have a hard time being enthusiastic if the person teaching them doesn't appear to be passionate about it themselves. Here's a list of "dos and don'ts" to help you with that:

**Don't** read your entire talk – no one expects you to be a master orator. However, try to avoid having to read your entire talk off sheets of paper. You'll spend most of your time looking down reading, rather than looking at your youth group. This will make the youth switch off and make it hard to convince them that what you're saying is relevant or that you really believe what you're saying. Instead, **do** use notes to prompt yourself, so that you don't forget the flow of your talk or miss any important points.

**Don't** overuse PowerPoint – adults get bored of lengthy PowerPoint presentations in business meetings, so why would youth be any different in youth meetings? If you wish to use PowerPoint, **do** keep the points brief or use images to illustrate your point. Your talk may be good for auditory learners, so using appropriate images or using brief points on

PowerPoint will help the visual learners. Limit PowerPoint usage to 10 minutes or less.

**Do** move about – when someone is passionate about a subject, they don't tend to sit still – they're more likely to walk about and use gestures. Do this yourself, rather than standing motionless (and emotionless) behind a lectern like a university professor. However, **don't** purely walk back and forth the front like you need to use the restroom.

**Do** vary your voice tone – when you're passionate about something, people can tell. Not only through your body language, but through your tone of voice as well. Therefore, **don't** talk in a monotone throughout your talk – express your passion for your message through your voice.

**Do** make good eye contact – looking at your group throughout the talk will make them think you're talking to them, helping your talk feel more relevant. **Don't** spend too much time looking down at your notes or off to the side while you think of what to say next.

When planning your talk, the thing to keep coming back to is *"What point am I trying to get across?"* This will help you to keep your focus on what you want to say, rather than going off on a tangent to something only vaguely linked to your intended message. Decide what you want your point to be, work out ways to get that message across and then analyze your talk to ensure you're sticking to your point.

## Worship
On a Christian youth retreat, a time for worship should be included in the main meetings. If you have a worship band who are able to lead worship at your meetings, that's great. If you don't have anybody who is able to lead worship, consider playing worship music loudly through speakers instead.

## Games
Using games during the meetings will help make them even more fun for the youth. Up-front games will have a small amount of young people (or adults) play a game for the rest of the youth to watch and cheer them on. Mixer games will have all the young people involved in the game, giving them an opportunity to mingle and possibly find out more about each other.

## Small groups
After the meeting, splitting off into smaller groups to discuss the talk is a good way to delve deeper into the theme of the youth retreat. These discussions should be facilitated by the other adults on the retreat to help keep the discussions on topic.

To assist the volunteers, provide some questions they can ask to get the young people talking. The questions should ideally be open questions which require the students to think about their answer, rather than simply asking 'Yes/No' questions. They should also be linked back to the question you ask yourself when preparing your talk – "What point am I trying to get across?" The discussions can then be guided around this main point.

For example, if your talk was about modern-day miracles, some questions to use in the discussion time might be, "How do you think God is performing miracles today?" and "What miracles have you seen happen?"

**Action Points:**

- *Meetings will probably be the main opportunity to address your theme, so make them count*
- *Communicate well with anyone contributing towards the meetings*
- *Make the meetings fun, interesting and passionate*

# 11

## FEEDBACK

Everyone hopes that the youth retreat they run has been a success, but you won't truly know that for sure unless you ask those who are actually in the know – the youth and volunteers on the retreat, as well as the young people's parents. At the end of the retreat, ask them to complete a feedback form so that you have a better idea of what worked and what didn't.

It's best to use a mix of both open and closed questions. Closed questions are ones that can be answered 'Yes' or 'No', or on a scale from 'Excellent' to 'Poor'. Open questions are those which ask the respondent to provide an answer which could in theory be anything, such as 'What would you like the focus of the next youth retreat to be?'

You can also use a mix of open and closed questions when covering just the one subject. For example, one question might be, 'How did you find the main meetings each day?' and ask them to rate it on a scale from 'Awesome' to 'Bored out of my mind'. The next question could then be 'If you responded "Bored out of my mind", what could we do to make it more interesting or relevant to you?'

Instead of using scales like 'Excellent' to 'Poor' or 'Awesome' to 'Bored out of my mind', you could use smiley faces for the youth to choose from.

The purpose of asking for this feedback should be so that you can learn what worked and what didn't. Therefore, one word of warning – you may not like what the feedback has to say! After you've put so much time and effort into the retreat, the last thing you want to hear is how a young person found it really dull or one of the volunteers didn't think you communicated very well. However, it's far better to know what didn't work so that you can fix it the next time you run a retreat, rather than running five retreats and having youth and volunteers not enjoy it but be too embarrassed to tell you so.

To help with this, don't read the feedback forms immediately. When they've been completed, put them in an envelope and leave them for a day or two. At the end of the retreat, you'll probably be exhausted, both physically and emotionally. Waiting a day or two will help you get some rest, so that when you read the feedback you'll be in a better frame of mind to take on board any criticism. This will help give you a sense of perspective and shouldn't be quite so discouraging. Remember – a good evaluation and review now will make planning for the next retreat much easier.

It can be easy to allow negative comments to seem bigger than they are. When reviewing the feedback forms, collate the responses to the closed questions so that you can see how many people answered the questions in a certain way. For example:

**What did you think of the speaking in the main meetings?**

Awesome – 2
Loved it – 7
Liked it – 3
Meh, it was OK – 1
Bored out of my mind – 1

When reading through the forms, the people that answered "Meh, it was OK" and "Bored out of my mind" will probably jump out of you, which may lead you to think that the meetings didn't go well. However, looking at the results objectively once collated, you would be able to see that 12 of the 14 youth gave positive answers about the talks in the meetings.

Follow up questions for those who didn't enjoy a certain thing about the retreat are helpful, as they provide some context and can help you tweak things at the next retreat. Using the example above, the next question asked should be 'If you responded "Bored out of my mind", what could we have done to make it more interesting or relevant to you?' If they answered 'We'd only just learned about Fruits of the Spirit at my last youth group before we moved here', you'd know the problem wasn't necessarily due to the way the meetings were run.

If their answer was instead "I didn't like how the speaker just read everything off a piece of paper and didn't ever look at us", it might be good to take that feedback on board and perhaps work on that skill. Just because only one person gave that feedback, it doesn't mean others wouldn't agree – it may be that they didn't want to hurt your feelings. "Negative" feedback can actually be positive if it means you can learn and improve what you do next time.

Receiving feedback from the volunteers can be just as important as feedback from the youth, especially if you want the volunteers to help at the next retreat! Some of the questions you ask them would be the same as those you ask the youth, but you should also ask questions relating specifically to their experience as volunteers, particularly concerning matters like communication and organization.

Another group to get feedback from is parents. The questions you ask will mostly be different to the ones you asked the youth and volunteers, but parents can provide invaluable feedback nonetheless.

Ask parents to complete the feedback form about a week after their child gets back from the youth retreat – this will enable you to also ask them questions like "How excited was your child when they returned?" and "What did your child share with you about what they learned?" Questions such as these will give you some idea of how much passion the youth have when they get home and what meetings or discussions had the most impact on them. Other questions to ask include "How was the communication leading up to the retreat?" and "Was there any more information you would have liked about the retreat?"

Getting feedback from parents will help you build relationships with them and involve them more with your youth work and their child's life when not at home. Asking for their feedback and opinions shows them that you take their views seriously and that you want to do all you can to provide positive experiences for their child. This will in turn encourage them to support what you do, support which may be invaluable in the future.

Sample **_Feedback forms_** are another of the free documents you get with this book. Depending on your youth retreat and the activities you do, you'll probably need to change some of the questions and add some of your own, but the samples provide a good starting point of questions to ask.

## *Action Points*

- *Get feedback from youth, volunteers and parents*
- *Ask both open and closed questions*
- *Don't take criticism personally – use it to improve the retreat next time*

# 12

# CONCLUSION

We've covered a lot in the past eleven chapters. We've looked at why identifying the reason(s) for running a youth retreat is important and how to recruit and manage volunteers.

Once you have some volunteers on board, you should use them and the youth to help identify a theme. Be SMART in creating objectives for identified aims and goals.

By creating a realistic budget, you can ensure the retreat is made affordable but priced accurately, which will help to choose an appropriate retreat center.

When promoting your youth retreat, consider traditional, multimedia and online promotion tools to maximize the number of youth able to register for the retreat. Youth that will be in attendance can also be a great asset when involved in the planning of the retreat.

One important step in the planning process is the completion of risk assessments, including identifying hazards, measuring their risk and implementing control measures to keep youth and leaders safe.

Being well prepared for meetings will help ensure aims and objectives are met, youth are engaged and volunteers are well informed about the content.

Finally, getting thorough feedback about the youth retreat from the youth, their parents and your volunteers will help you evidence the learning outcomes and growth achieved throughout the retreat.

Now that the retreat is over, it's now probably about 6 – 12 months before your next youth retreat. Use everything you've learned from this book, the free templates provided and check our website for updates – http://youthworkinit.com/blog/ – to ensure that each of your retreats is better than the last!

# ABOUT THE AUTHORS

Stephen & Shae Pepper are the founders of Youth Workin' It, an organization that provides consultancy and services for youth workers and organizations worldwide.

On a personal level, we got married in 2004 and currently live in Portsmouth, Virginia. Stephen is English and Shae is American, so while reading this book you may find some of the terms unusual. If you're in the UK, it's probably an Americanism, while if you're in the US, it's probably an Englishism (neither of which are probably words). If you're somewhere else, who knows!

At Youth Workin' It, we provide advice, tips, opinions, ideas and resources relating to youth work and youth ministry throughout the week on our blog – all for free. You can subscribe to receive our blog posts each day via email – go to http://youthworkinit.com/blog/ and enter your email address in the "Subscribe to our Blog Posts" box.

You can follow @youthworkinit on Twitter and Like us at http://www.facebook.com/youthworkinit

Made in the USA
Monee, IL
02 January 2020